# WORKING DOGS

BY M.G. HIGGINS

# WHITE LIGHTNING
## BOOKS®
# NONFICTION

EDUCATIONAL PUBLISHING
www.sdlback.com

**Photo credits:** page 17: Photo 12/Alamy Stock Photo; pages 24/25: Belish/Shutterstock.com; page 28: Everett Collection Historical/Alamy Stock Photo; page 35: Glynnis Jones/Shutterstock.com

ISBN: 978-1-68021-741-4
eBook: 978-1-63078-911-4

Printed in Malaysia

24 23 22 21 20   1 2 3 4 5

# Table of Contents

# On the Job

In a field, a man stands with his dog. He whistles at her. She runs after a flock of sheep. The sheep go where she guides them. The man whistles again. This time, his tone is different. The dog runs back to the man's side.

It is a busy day in the city. A woman walks with her dog. They stop at a crosswalk. Cars zoom by. Then the light changes. Now it is safe for them to go. The dog steps onto the street. He leads the woman across. She cannot see, so the dog is her guide.

There are 90 million dogs in the U.S. Most have one role. They are pets. Others have jobs like these two.

Working dogs have special talents. Some are natural **traits**. One is a strong sense of smell. Search dogs rely on this. They sniff for missing people. Chasing **prey** is another skill. Herding dogs chase **livestock**.

**FAST FACT:** The average dog is as smart as a two-year-old child.

# Eager to Please

Most dogs want to please. They are **pack animals**. This means they live in groups. Dogs obey a leader. That is the alpha dog. A working dog sees its owner as the alpha. They want to do what their owner says. This makes them easy to train.

Puppies are born with many skills. They must be trained to work. This is not hard. Most are smart. They can learn hundreds of commands. Trainers offer rewards. Food is one. A toy is another. Play is often the biggest reward.

**FAST FACT:** A favorite game dogs play with their trainers is tug-of-war.

## HAPPY DOGS

Not all people like their jobs. It can be the same with dogs. A good match is important. Energetic dogs are good for herding. They are not as good for therapy. Calm dogs are better for that. Studies show that most dogs like their work. This is a good thing for people. Dogs have been helping them for a very long time.

CHAPTER

2

# The Origin of Dogs

It was thousands of years ago. Early humans lived together. They made camp. A trash pile started. Gray wolves nosed around it. The animals wanted an easy meal. Some growled at people and bared their teeth. Most wolves were a threat. Men chased them away.

One small wolf did not growl. Many liked her. They fed her scraps. She stayed and had pups. The pups lived with the people too. These wolves became tame.

Is this where dogs came from? Scientists are not sure. More research is needed.

## Helping Humans

The change to **domesticated** dog took time. Ears got floppy. Coats had more spots. **Personalities** changed. Dogs learned to obey humans. They lived together. People became their new packs.

**FAST FACT:** Scientists are not sure where dogs got their start. It could have been Europe or the Middle East. Others think it was East Asia.

Dogs have sharp senses. One is smell. Another is hearing. Early people put these traits to work. Many took dogs on hunts. They tracked and chased prey. People caught more food.

Over time, people **evolved**. They gave dogs new jobs. People kept herds. Sheep were valuable. Dogs guarded them. Men used dogs in war too. These dogs attacked enemies. Others kept watch. They barked to scare strangers away.

People began to **breed** dogs. Certain traits were encouraged. Breeds were matched to jobs. Big dogs scared enemies. Smaller ones chased rats. Lap dogs were bred too. These like to be near people.

Dogs still do old jobs. They have new ones too. Their sharp senses help them in every role.

**FAST FACT:** Dogs might have been domesticated from wolves. But they are now a different species.

## IN SYNC

Studies show that dogs understand human emotions. They can read people's faces and voices. Dogs can even smell when a person is scared. This makes them good pets. It also makes them good at working with people.

# Police Dogs

A crime takes place. Witnesses call the police. The criminal runs away. He is fast. Officers cannot keep up. But Max can.

The dog closes in. He bites the man's arm. The man screams and hits. Max holds on. Finally, his partner arrives. She commands the dog to let go. Together, they catch the criminal.

Max is a police dog. Police have used dogs for centuries. This started in Europe. U.S. police began using dogs in the 1970s.

Certain breeds make good police dogs. One is the most common. That is the German shepherd. These dogs are smart. They work hard too.

**FAST FACT:** Just seeing a police dog keeps many criminals from being violent.

# Training for the Force

Each dog has a human partner. These partners are in control. Dogs learn to obey their commands. Sometimes they are in English. Often they are in another language. Why? Many police dogs come from Europe. Their partners use words they know. Dogs also recognize their partner's voice. A bond forms between the pair.

**FAST FACT:** Most police dogs wear badges. These attach to a collar or harness.

## ANOTHER NAME

A police dog is also called a K-9. This is a shortened version of *canine*, another word for dog. The U.S. Army called its War Dogs program during World War II the "K-9 Corps." The term became popular after that.

Police dogs do many tasks. Some are like Max. They chase and catch criminals. Many do scent work. These dogs sniff for drugs or bombs. They find people. A few even smell where a fire started.

Training these dogs is expensive. It costs thousands. This is just in the beginning. Most need more training later. Not all forces can afford dogs. Many rely on **grants**.

Police dogs train as puppies. At 18 months, they start working. Most work for around seven years. They live with their partner. That is their home after they retire too. Then they are treated like pets.

**FAST FACT:** Beagles make good sniffers. They smell bags at airports for drugs or bombs.

# Herding Dogs

Livestock are on the move. One cow breaks from the herd. A collie chases it. He snaps at the cow's heels. Sharp hooves just miss his head. The dog snaps again. Finally the cow returns to the group.

The collie has done his job. He has kept the cattle together.

For dogs, herding is an old job. It relies on two **instincts**. One is stalking prey. The other is chasing it. This likely started with hunts. Dogs went along with people. Their powerful senses were useful. Finding **game** became easier. People did not let dogs eat it. They made dogs bring it back. Hunters offered rewards. This taught dogs to herd.

**FAST FACT:** There are about 30 breeds of herding dogs.

## AM I A GOAT?

One herder's job is guard duty. That is the Great Pyrenees. It can weigh over 100 pounds. This big dog chases coyotes. Wolves run from it too. The puppies are not raised with people. They grow up with goats or sheep. These dogs bond with the animals. Their instinct to protect them is strong.

# Protecting the Herd

Herders keep livestock together. They move them to fresh grass. Some bring back strays. Sheep sometimes wander. Cows can get stuck in mud. Roads are dangerous. Animals might get lost. Dogs get them to safety.

There are many ways to herd. Cattle are large. Controlling them is hard. But dogs know what to do. **Nipping** a heel does the trick. A bite on the nose can too. Dogs get in front of sheep. They stare them down. Sheep fear dogs. Most run where they are chased.

Many breeds do this work. One is the border collie. Another is the corgi.

These dogs are smart. They love working. Having a job makes them happy. Keeping them as pets is challenging. The dogs might try to herd people. Kids and adults get rounded up. Herders need to stay active. Lying around is not for them.

**FAST FACT:** Herding trials are popular. These are contests. Dogs and their handlers compete to be the best.

# CHAPTER 5

# Search and Rescue Dogs

Thick snow covers a mountain. Then it begins to slide. This is an **avalanche**. People ski out of the way. Not all make it. One woman is buried in the snow. Her air will run out in minutes. She must get out.

**FAST FACT:** Dogs can smell a human under 15 feet of snow.

This victim is lucky. Duke is on the job. He finds her scent. The dog digs until he reaches her. Rescuers pull her out.

Duke does search and rescue (SAR). These dogs work hard. One can do the work of 20 people. Many search in snow. Others search in forests. Some work in cities. Their goal is the same. They want to find a missing person.

Sometimes a victim cannot be saved. Dogs still have a job to do. They find the body. This helps the family. Now their loved one can be buried.

## Tracking Scents

These dogs use their sense of smell. Dogs can smell things people cannot. Their noses are sensitive. Each person has their own scent. It comes from skin cells. The cells fall off. They land on the ground. Or they float in the air. This is what dogs sniff for.

SAR dogs search in two ways. One is tracking. Handlers take the dog to the search area. This is where someone was last seen. The dog sniffs something the person wore. It follows the smell along the ground. Skin cells leave a trail. But tracking must happen fast. Trails disappear quickly.

Air sniffing is another way. These dogs do not need to smell clothes. They sniff for a scent. Then they find its source.

**FAST FACT:** A person has 6 million scent glands. A dog has up to 300 million. A dog's sense of smell can be 10,000 to 100,000 times stronger than a person's.

The best breeds are brave. Some may need to climb ladders. Others are lowered down cliffs. Obeying is important. At times there is danger. Disaster zones change quickly. A building could fall. The earth might shake. Dogs must follow commands. This keeps them safe.

## 9/11 HEROES

A terrible attack happened in New York City. The date was September 11, 2001. Planes flew into two tall buildings. The buildings fell. Many people were hurt or killed. Some were trapped in the rubble. Air sniffing dogs were fast on the scene. About 300 worked at the site. Their shifts could last 12 hours. The dogs saved lives. They became heroes.

A dog's size matters too. Dogs might dig through **debris**. Large dogs do best in rubble. They can push things out of the way. Smaller dogs are easier to transport. Work sites can be far away.

SAR work is all about play. Searching is a game for these dogs. Finding someone is the reward.

**FAST FACT:** Hounds make good trackers. Their long ears direct scents toward the nose.

# Service Dogs

Jin falls in her home. She cannot get up. Buck runs to her side. The dog stiffens. Jin braces her hands on his back. This lets her push up and stand. They have done this before. An illness makes Jin tired. She often loses her balance. It is hard for her to get around. Buck is a service dog. He helps in many ways.

**FAST FACT:** Service dogs help disabled people live independent lives.

Buck wears a harness. On top is a handle. Jin holds it as they walk. It keeps her steady. He picks up items she drops. Sometimes Jin's legs hurt. The dog lies on them. This eases her pain. He even helps change sheets. Buck has 75 skills in all.

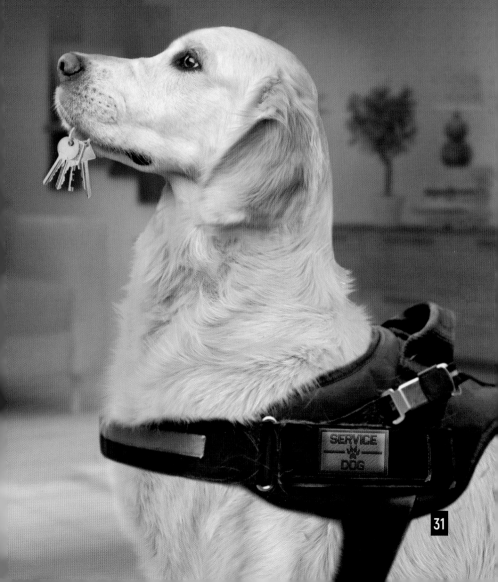

# Always on Duty

Many service dogs help deaf people. They alert owners to sounds. A knock on the door is one. Another is a smoke alarm. The dog knows what to do for each sound.

The first service dogs may have been guides. An old drawing was found. It was on a wall in Rome. In it, a dog leads a blind man. Today guide dogs help in traffic. Dogs act like a person's eyes. They stop at curbs and steps. Safety is their goal.

Laws protect service dogs. Most businesses do not allow animals. But service dogs can go in stores. Restaurants let them in. They go on airplanes too. The people they help need them.

Training can take two years. Dogs start with basic commands. Special skills come next. They use these on the job. Then the owner meets the dog. There is more training together.

Retrievers make good service dogs. But any breed will do. Some come from shelters. Others are from breeders. The dogs need to be social. They should be smart too. There is much to learn. Each dog needs different skills. These depend on the person.

## PRISON DOGS

Some service dogs start out in prison. Prisons have training programs. Inmates work with puppies. They teach them basic skills. These programs are a success. People in need get a trained dog. Inmates learn new skills. One is trust. Few of these inmates end up back in prison.

# How to Interact with a Service Dog

Service dogs attract attention when they are out. They may look friendly, but they are also doing important jobs for their owners. These dogs should not be distracted. Here are some guidelines to follow when you see a service dog wearing a vest.

| DO | DON'T |
|---|---|
| Talk to the owner, not the dog. | Make sounds or whistle at the dog. |

| DO | DON'T |
|---|---|
| Follow the owner's instructions. | Pet the dog without asking first. |

| **DO** | **DON'T** |
|---|---|
| Keep your own dog a safe distance away. | Offer food or treats to the dog. |
| **DO** | **DON'T** |
| Treat the dog's owner with respect. | Ask the owner personal questions. |
| **DO** | **DON'T** |
| Remember that the dog is working. | Get in the way of the dog and its owner. |

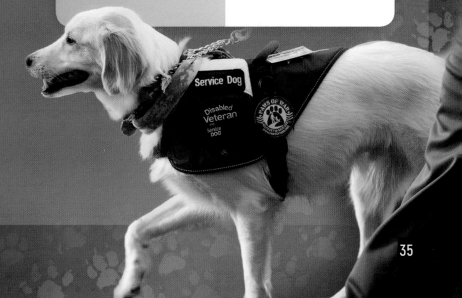

Service Dog

Disabled Veteran and Service DOG

PAWS OF WAR

# 7 Therapy Dogs

Avi is a little boy. He is in the hospital. The nurses are nice. But he misses his friends and family. One day a woman visits. She brings a dog. Its name is Bit. The pup licks Avi's face. He laughs and pets it. For a moment he feels happy.

Bit is a therapy dog. More than 50,000 work in the U.S. These are not service dogs. Service dogs help their owners. Therapy dogs help others. Hospitals use them. Nursing homes do too. Their job is to interact. People pet and hold them. Owners guide the dog. They direct how it behaves.

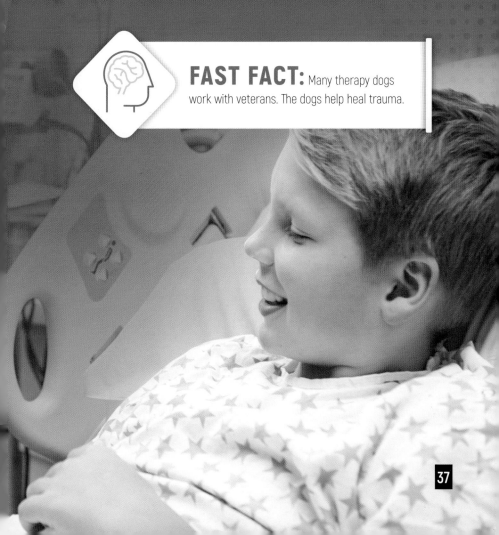

**FAST FACT:** Many therapy dogs work with veterans. The dogs help heal trauma.

# Classroom Assistants

Students may not read well. Schools have programs to help. A dog sits with them. They read to it. The animal listens. It does not judge. This helps readers relax. Readers gain confidence.

There is another school program. It helps kids build trust. A girl talks to a dog. She shares her feelings. The animal listens and does not blame. The girl learns social skills. **Empathy** grows too.

Experts have done studies. These dogs can improve health. Stress levels go down. Blood pressure drops. It is good for the dogs too. They relax when people pet them.

**FAST FACT:** Disaster relief dogs comfort people after a crisis. They go to disaster zones to offer emotional support.

Any breed can do this job. Some traits are important. The dog must be friendly. It needs to like people. Staying calm is big. Groups may test dogs. They look for these traits. A dog that has them gets certified. Anyone can train a therapy dog. Often the owner does it.

## EMOTIONAL SUPPORT

Some people get upset easily. Pet dogs help keep them calm. These are emotional support dogs. Any dog can be one. Owners take them many places. Some people like the idea. The animals help owners cope. Others point to issues. Few of these dogs get formal training. They do not always behave well in public. Laws do not allow these dogs in all the places service dogs can go.

# CHAPTER 8

# Medical Detection Dogs

Zip is curled up at Val's feet. But they are not at home. Val is at school. The dog sniffs the air. He jumps up. Val feels a wet nose on her hand. It is a warning. She feels fine, but Zip is always right.

They hurry to see the nurse. He tests Val's blood. Her **blood sugar** is low. She could have passed out. Val pats her dog's head. Zip has helped her again.

Val has **diabetes**. This makes her blood sugar unstable. Blood sugar changes can cause problems. She can feel sick. Or she might pass out. Early **detection** is important. But symptoms are hard to notice. By then it may be too late.

## Sniffing Out Sickness

Dogs sense issues much sooner. The body changes when someone is ill. It gives off a scent. People cannot smell it. Dogs can. An odor is in the breath. Sweat has it too.

Training teaches the dog what to notice. First it learns the basics. Then it trains with its new owner. It learns the owner's scents. Some odors are normal. The dog ignores those. Another smell means the person is sick. That scent makes the dog act. It gives an alert. Often this is a nudge.

Dogs help people who have **seizures** too. These can happen without warning. The person could fall. They could get hurt.

**FAST FACT:** Dogs can warn someone of a seizure up to 45 minutes before it happens.

**FAST FACT:** Cancer detection dogs can sniff 300 samples a day. Some have a 98% success rate.

A dog can sense a seizure. This is well before it happens. Experts are not sure how. There could be a change in smell. It might be something else. These animals alert their owners. Now the person can get to a safe place. That could be a bed or couch.

There is a new medical trend. Dogs sniff out cancer. So far they only work in labs. That could change in the future. These dogs work fast. They make few mistakes.

## MORE ANIMAL DETECTORS

Other animals detect disease too. Pigeons have sharp eyesight. They can pick out cancer cells on X-rays. Mice sniff bird droppings to find bird flu. Rats sniff for tuberculosis. Fruit flies can find cancer cells. They "smell" it with their feelers.

# CHAPTER 9

# Dogs in Entertainment

Not all dogs have jobs like that. Some are less serious.

A soldier comes home. He was gone a long time. His dog runs to greet him. It wags its tail and licks his face. The moment is sweet. Cameras catch it. But this is not really the man's dog. Both are actors. They work together. This is for an advertisement.

The first dogs to entertain did not act. They fought. People watched and made bets. Many dogs got hurt. Now most countries ban dog fighting. Dogs entertain in other ways. They are in films and TV shows. Ads use them too.

## DOG MASCOTS

Mascots are symbols. Many sports teams have them. They boost pep and pride. Sometimes mascots are people in costumes. In college football, more than 30 are live dogs. Bulldogs are popular. Huskies are too. These dogs need little training. Most hang out on the sidelines. Some might go to special events. Wearing a costume is often part of the job.

**FAST FACT:** Dog racing was once a popular form of entertainment in the U.S. Just a few states still allow it.

# Furry Celebrities

It was the 1920s. Movies with dogs were a big hit. One star was Rin Tin Tin. He was a German shepherd. The dog starred in many films. Fans sent him thousands of letters a week.

Lassie was another famous dog. She was in movies and TV shows. These came out over several decades. The collie was supposed to be female. But more than one dog played her. The most well-known was male. His real name was Pal. He was in seven movies. They were big hits. Pal earned a lot of money. In one film, the human star made less. The dog did not keep the money. It went to his trainer.

Dogs still act in many roles. Stars come in all sizes and breeds. They can be mutts too. These dogs are a mix of breeds. One famous mutt was Benji. He was in many movies. Benji always came to the rescue.

**FAST FACT:** Rin Tin Tin's nickname was Rinty. He lived to be 14 years old.

Good acting dogs share some skills. They behave well. Being intelligent is key. Most commands are silent. Noise cannot end up on film. Trainers use hand signs. They might signal with their eyes and face. Basic commands include sit and stay. There are many more.

Certain scenes take special talent. Dogs need to show emotion. Maybe a dog in a movie gets injured. She must limp and whine. Later the dog has to look sad. She puts her head down. Her ears go back. A scary film needs a mean dog. The dog bares his teeth. He growls. These dogs tell the story.

The best human actors look natural. People forget they are acting. It is the same with dogs. The best are realistic.

# More Famous Movie Dogs

| Movie | Role | Dog Star | Breed |
| --- | --- | --- | --- |
| *The Wizard of Oz* (1939) | Toto | Terry | Cairn Terrier |
| *Turner and Hooch* (1989) | Hooch | Beasley | French Mastiff |
| *Beethoven* (1992) | Beethoven | Chris | St. Bernard |
| *Air Bud* (1997) | Buddy | Buddy | Golden Retriever |
| *Harry Potter and the Sorceror's Stone* (2001) | Fang | Hugo | Neapolitan Mastiff |

# Dogs with Unique Jobs

Most have heard of police dogs. Herders are common too. Service dogs are seen all over. But some dogs have unique jobs. They help in special ways.

Piper works at an airport. He does not sniff luggage. This dog works outside. The border collie scans the runway. His ears perk up. Geese land nearby. The dog takes off. He frightens the geese away. Now the runway is safe.

Chasing birds is Piper's job. He chases rodents too. This is because they attract birds. At airports, birds cause problems. They can **collide** with planes. That can damage planes. They might even crash. Dogs keep the runway clear. Not many dogs do this job. But their work is important.

**FAST FACT:** Dogs have been trained to sniff for diseases that kill bees.

Some dogs are divers. Lila is one. She swims down 15 feet. A lobster is below. The dog grabs it with her mouth. Up she swims. Her owner gets to have lobster for dinner. He trained Lila to dive for them.

Swimming dogs have more jobs. It is a hot day at the beach. People wade in the ocean. A swimmer is in trouble. She waves her arms. The lifeguard swims out. A dog paddles with him. This dog is a lifeguard too. They reach the swimmer. She holds on to the dog. It guides her back to shore. These dogs save lives.

Dogs use their noses for other jobs. Police need assistance. They bring Bear inside a house. The dog sniffs around. Bear gives a signal. He has found something. This is not a person or drugs. It is a flash drive. Someone hid it in a wall. Bear sniffs just for electronics. That could be a computer. It might be a chip. The data on them can crack a case.

**FAST FACT:** Italy has more than 350 lifeguard dogs. Some can pull up to six people to shore at one time.

# Creative Pups

A few dogs are artists. One dog takes a brush in her mouth. She dips it in paint. The mutt moves her head. It sways from side to side. Color goes on the canvas. This takes about ten minutes. Then the painting is complete.

This dog was a rescue. Her owners adopted her from a shelter. She picked up tricks fast. Keeping her busy was tough. They tried teaching her to paint. The dog learned it right away. Some paintings sell for over $400. Proceeds go to a charity for animals.

Most dogs are beloved pets. That is an important role. But some dogs do much more. They work with police. Herders manage animals on farms. Therapy dogs give comfort. Other dogs sniff out diseases. These dogs work to make life better for people.

# PRICELESS

Several dogs work as artists. Some use brushes. Others use different tools. One claws at the canvas. Another steps in paint. Then he leaves paw prints. Dog art can be pricey. Some pieces sell for over $1,000.

# Glossary

**avalanche:** a large amount of snow that suddenly slides down a mountain

**blood sugar:** a source of energy in a person's body; also known as glucose

**breed:** to choose a male and female animal of a certain kind for the purpose of having babies

**collide:** to bump or crash into

**debris:** broken pieces left after something is destroyed

**detection:** the act of discovering something

**diabetes:** a disease where the body cannot use sugar normally

**domesticated:** made tame over time; no longer wild

**empathy:** the ability to understand and share someone else's feelings

**evolve:** to develop into something more advanced over time

**game:** animals hunted for food

**grant:** money given to someone for a specific purpose

**instinct:** a way of thinking or behaving that has not been taught

**livestock:** farm animals

**nip:** to bite gently

**pack animal:** an animal that lives and hunts in a group

**personality:** what someone tends to act like

**prey:** an animal that is hunted and killed by another animal

**seizure:** a medical condition where someone's body moves in uncontrollable ways

**trait:** a quality that helps describe how a person or animal looks or acts

# TAKE A LOOK INSIDE
# DEADLY BITES

# CHAPTER 5

## Forest and Ice

Some think bears are cute. They look like stuffed animals. Because of that, some think they must be harmless. This is not accurate. Bears kill.

### Grizzly Bears

Grizzlies are a kind of brown bear. They used to fear people. That changed over 50 years ago. National Parks had open garbage pits. Campers kept food near tents. Bears started to scavenge for food. They got close to people. Bears stopped being scared.

One attacked on August 13, 1967. This was at Glacier National Park. The bear killed a woman. An attack had not happened in the park's history of more than 50 years. Something about that day was strange, though. A few hours later, there was a second attack. A different bear hurt another woman.

**FAST FACT:** About 20,000 grizzlies live in Canada. Alaska has about 30,000. Only about 1,800 live in the rest of the U.S. Most of those are in national parks.

# Small and Deadly

Big animals kill people. Some small ones do too. **Venom** is one of the tools they use. It packs a deadly punch.

## Snakes

There are over 3,000 kinds of snakes in the world. A fifth of those use venom. Snakes use it to take down prey. They also use it in self-defense. People are not prey to these snakes. They just pose a danger. A person may surprise a snake. Someone may try to handle one. The snake wants to be left alone. It bites.

The inland Taipan lives in Australia. It has the strongest venom. One dose can kill 100 people. But the snake is shy. It would rather get away than fight. That keeps it from biting many.

**FAST FACT:** A gland near a snake's eye stores venom. A muscle pushes the liquid down the fangs.

---

# Killers That Don't Bite

Not all animals kill with bites. Some killers don't even have teeth. They are bugs.

## Mosquitoes

One bug kills more than all others. It is the mosquito. They can carry disease. One is malaria. Yellow fever is another. The Zika virus is deadly too. These illnesses and others kill approximately 725,000 people each year. They make millions sick. Mosquitoes live all over the world. There are a few places without them. Most live in Africa and Asia.

Why are these bugs so deadly? One reason is how they eat. Females drink blood. They land on a person. Then they stab the skin with a tiny tube. It is like a needle. The tube gets blood. Germs get picked up too. Then the bug lands on the next person. The germs get passed on.

There is another reason for deaths. It is the number of these bugs. There are billions. They like warm and moist climates best. That describes many places.

**FAST FACT:** Mosquitoes are not all bad. They are food for many animals. Bats, birds, and frogs depend on them.

# WH/TE L/GHTNING
## BOOKS®
## NONFICTION

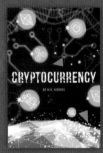

CRYPTOCURRENCY
BY M.G. HIGGINS

9781680216387

DEADLY BITES

9781680216400

DIGITAL WORLDS
BY EMILY SCHLESINGER

9781680217377

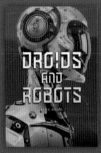

DROIDS AND ROBOTS
BY M.G. HIGGINS

9781680216394

ESPORTS

9781680217391

FLIGHT SQUADS
BY EMILY SCHLESINGER

9781680216912

OLYMPIC GAMES
BY M.G. HIGGINS

9781680217384

WORKING DOGS
BY M.G. HIGGINS

9781680217414

WORLD CUP SOCCER
BY EMILY SCHLESINGER

9781680217407

## MORE TITLES COMING SOON
SDLBACK.COM/WHITE-LIGHTNING-BOOKS